SAP Business Workflow Interview Questions, Answers, and Explanations

SAPCOOKBOOK.COM

Please visit our website at www.sapcookbook.com

ISBN 1-933804-05-X

Trademark notices

TABLE OF CONTENTS

SAP Business Workflow Interview Questions

Part I: SAP Business Workflow FAQ

Question 1: Clarification on PR Item release

For a PR Item level release, the standard workflow works like this:

For a 3 level release, the workflow goes from level 1 to level 3. In case of any rejections in-between, the rejection workflow goes back to Level 1, who will then release the refusal. This will send the workflow back to the level it was rejected at.

The requirement is now to make the workflow go in the exact reverse order, i.e.
Once Level 3 rejects, workflow goes back to level 2;
When Level 2 resets its release and rejects, workflow goes back to Level 1;
When Level 1 resets its release, makes the necessary changes, and resubmits the PR, it flows up to level 2;
And so forth.

Is this scenario possible with the standard workflow and BUS2009 events?

A: If there is a rejection at any point, you can utilize the workflow release strategy. This will enable the release on a step by step level. For example:

If rejected at 3;
Reset strategy to initial level.

If released at 1 in background;
Go to 2 and stop.

You will need to keep track of the value where it was rejected. From there,
you can then create your own custom method for that based in the bus2009.singlerelease.

Question 2: Undelete Work items

Undelete Work items in SAP workflow

Is there anyway to undelete work items in SAP workflow after I have logically deleted them already?

A. No. What you can do is restart the workflow using SWUE. This will be the same as recreating the workflow because it will start at the point where it has logically been deleted.

Question 3: Workflow completing prematurely

WF starts on creating a Service notification IW51 BUS obj 2080 -- method Create.

This works fine in starting the Workflow. However, I only want the workflow to register completion when the notification is set at CLOSED (Bus 2080 event CLOSED). This is because I have an asynchronous edit task with a terminating function CLOSED.

Usually, the original and current setup works fine (for example if anybody executes IW52 outside the normal workflow the workflow is marked complete).
However if any of the agents execute a the work item in the inbox and don't close the notification -i.e. just to come in and edit the notification (IW52) without closing the notification properly, the work item still is marked complete.

This should not happen until the notification is closed.

Is there any way to re-submit the work item to the inbox for completion?

A. Add a 'loop until' to the step that is sent to the agent and program to loop until the status is CLOSED. If the status is not closed after the agent processes, then your WF will loop back to the step that sends the work item to the respective agent.

Question 4: ESS Leave request

I encountered an issue while executing an ESS employee leave request (WS20000081). To explain further, when an employee creates a leave request through ESS, it goes to his manager. If the request is logon to R/3 and his manager approves the leave request through the same R/3 workplace, the request goes back out from that screen. This scenario works fine. However, the problem starts when I do the same request from his manager's portal and I press the "Approve" button, I get the message saying "Information sent successfully". I will then press the "OK" button, and then press the button "Quit". When I double checked, the workflow is still sitting at the manager's inbox. My question is why doesn't this work from the manager's portal when the same function is working inside the R/3?

A.   If you are approving from the ESS which is deployed in Enterprise Portal, you should also deploy Universal Work List. It is only then that the Leave Approvals will work properly.

Question 5: Pop up message for workflow

How do you set up a user to receive a pop-up reminder when he/she gets a new WF message?

A. You can accomplish this by setting up the work item priority to the highest level.

Question 6: Timed events

Is it possible to create timed events?

A. You may consider using deadline monitoring facilities. For example:

Requested start, requested end;

Latest start or latest end on tasks;

Apply whichever may be applicable to your case.

Question 7: User Alternative in Workflow

Can I define (or assign) an alternative person in the workflow? For example if I delete a user who is in my workflow list, is it possible that the slot for the workflow be diverted to an alternate user?

A corollary question is - is it also possible to substitute a user who has been deleted by another user without the workflow getting affected? If this is possible, how can this be achieved?

A. You can setup substitution rules but not for deleted userIDs. Generally, substitutions are setup by the person who needs to be replaced (and only for a period of time). I think your best solution is to define a RULE that looks for the userID. If it's not valid, then build some additional logic that tells it who to look for next. Of course, a more central solution is to define a 'WORKCENTER' HR object and assign all the possible agents to this work center. Then set this work center as the agent of the task.

Question 8: Workflow for PB40

How do you set the workflow in the transaction PB40 of HR for functional mobility?

A. The only standard WF that comes close is 200038 but it could be too robust for what you are trying to achieve. You may want to create your own WF and (at some point) call the method APPLICANT-EVENTCREATE. This method is similar to PB40 but without the first screen.

Question 9: Plant Maintenance Notification

I am currently using a standard task TS 00008314 (BUS2038) to launch work flow when notification is created. Given this, how can I define notification type (only M1)? Subsequently, how I can launch a pop up or express message when notification is created.

A. You can create a start condition (transaction: SWB_COND) and set it to start if the notification type is M1. Just make sure to document this because months from now you might not remember why it starts selectively for some and not others.

For the second question - if you are trying to notify the agent that they have a task, then try placing this standard task into a custom 2 step workflow template. The first step of the template should send an express mail then the next step should automatically send the task.

Question 10: Downloading Workflows

Is it possible to download my workflows?

A. Yes it is. From the workflow builder menu, choose Workflow > Import/Export and export to an XML file. You can also import from an XML file into a different system in which case the builder will create a new workflow in a 'New, Not Saved' status. Then when you save it, it will assign the unique IDs for the workflow and each task.

You might also consider getting the program logic for any custom business objects. You can do this by going to the basic data of the business object and double-click the program name. From here, you can choose download from the utilities menu to get the program which includes the custom methods, attributes, etc.

Question 11: User assignment

Maintaining user assignment in standard role – extending assignment date

It is a policy in our company that the Security Department extends the user validity period of each user ID every year end i.e. from 12.31.2005 to 12.31.2006. We have to do this manually every year and this year, I was trying to find out how to assign the validity period to a much later date than the usual annual cut off. Is there a better way to configure this without going through each user ID manually?

A. You can follow these steps:
1. Go to transaction PSO4 (Maintain Infotype);
2. Then go to Object Type - RY (Responsibility);
3. Proceed to Object ID - This is the organizational id of your responsibility. The abbreviation will be the same as that of your rule. Use F4 to get the ID.
4. Execute and change the infotype, selecting 1001 (Relationships). Change the validity here.
Lastly, you might need to wrap the whole operation in a BDC or something for automation.

Question 12: Position Basis

Is Workflow position based?

Is it true that workflow is position based and not person based? Does it mean that when a user quits a job, the workflow will not be affected?

A. Yes, Workflow is position based. Therefore any turnover will not affect the workflow unless the person who has quit the job is the only person for the position you are talking about. Check the transaction as reference for PPOCE/PPOME for organizational structures.

Question 13: Approval workflow

I would like to implement the SAP Standard Workflow for the release of purchase acquisitions. I have access to OSS but I need a detailed guide in implementing the SAP standard. Is there documentation for the configuration of an Approval Workflow?

A. There is an SAP Online help that you can use for a detailed documentation in configuring an Approval Workflow. You can use this link:

http://help.sap.com/saphelp_46c/helpdata/en/33/4c9a34272a5f2ee10000009b38f83b/frameset.htm

In the first chapter, "Releasing a Purchase Requisition", there is technical information, process overview and the standard SAP workflows for the purchase release process. This will start you off.

Question 14: Remove object type

I have created a situation wherein the 'Z' object in 'SWO1' was transposed to 'obsolete' by mistake. After this, I am not able to edit the object anymore. This message appears each time I try to delete the obsolete misstep:

"Obsolete object types cannot be changed again."

How can I reverse the mistake?

A. You can change the status in table TOJTB > Field OBSOLETE and the object can be edited again. However, this is not recommended and there might be unknown implications.

Question 15: Workflow for releasing requisitions

I am currently working on creating a release procedure with workflow for requisitions purposes. I have completed the release strategies and formulated an organizational plan. I was able to maintain the workflow parameters in transaction OMGQ. For each release code I used object type position (S) and I assigned the corresponding position ID from the organizational plan. When I pose a requisition, the strategy seems to be correctly assigned. However, workflow itself is not activated. Are there any more settings that I need to maintain to activate SAP standard workflow for releasing requisitions?

In my business workplace I see the message:

"Workflow Wizard 'DYNAMICHIERARCHICAL': Create initialization."

When I double clicked on this message I get the error message:

"Prefix number: entry missing for system DEV".

How do I resolve this issue?

A. You will need to do two things to fix this.

1. Run AUTOMATIC customizing;

2. You need to define the prefix numbers for the workflow definition time;

Question 16: Alternative Approvers

How can I re-route a PO/PR to an alternate approver?

A. Go to "Latest end" tab in workflow step properties. From there set the deadline parameters including a recipient for missed deadline items. Alternatives will then be set.

Question 17: Workflow not triggered

How do I ensure that training and event workflow is automatically triggered? When I test the object through SWUE, I am able to see the event log. However, it is not getting through T Code. I also tried it in SWE2 but I got the same results. How can this be configured correctly?

A. You already started troubleshooting in the right track. Continue on and check the linkage if it is active or not. After that, it will trigger automatically.

Question 18: Workflow sent to Every Agent

Why are workflow items sent to everyone if agent is not determined?

Why is it that the workflow items are sent to everyone if agent is not specified?

I tried to go thru "PFTC_CHG" transaction by specifying the task (20000460), and under "default values" Tab, the agent is defined with rule 157.

What other steps do I need to take to clarify the tasks?

A. This is generally a two part issue and there are two possible solutions:

1. Instead of making it a general task, try to identify an actual list of 'possible' agents. This could be based positions, user IDs, Org Units, etc. Make this list your possible agents instead of defining it as a general task.

Or:

2. Make sure your logic for determining the agent always returns an agent. If you are using a custom

rule, then at the end of the logic check to see if an agent was determined and if not, identify a default agent (like a WF admin or business analyst) that can receive the item and investigate who to properly route it to.

Note: If you go with option 1 and at runtime the logic fails to determine an agent, then an error message is sent to the WF admin instead of the task being sent to everyone.

Question 19: Adding functions

Adding a function module - How and Where

How do I configure a pop-up box to appear to notify the approver when a message is sent to his inbox?

A. Change the priority of the step to 'Highest' in the 'Other' tab.

Question 20: Inbox display-Transaction

Our company is in the process of customizing enduser screen using SAP GUIxt.
I have to call the workflow 'inboxscreen' only. I tried to use SWBP and SO01 TRANSACTION. However, I have to display the inbox message only. How can this be done?

A. In your custom program set the parameters for type and ID (sap transaction. SWI5) and call the same transaction, using call transaction statement.

Use the Type US and assign ID as its user name.

Question 21: Transferring User Outbox

We need to change the username of one of the users on our system. Simultaneously, she would like to take all of her work items, completed and uncompleted onto this new account with her. We were able to forward the uncompleted items from her inbox using SWIA. However, we can't find a way to forward the contents of the outbox. Is there a way to resolve this?

A. This is not usually done. However, you can try to work around this. Create one abap report based on transaction .SWI5 and SWI14. Use transparent tables SWWWIHEAD, SWWWLOGHIST and some more, which will display all work item executed by that user.

Question 22: Approval Users

Capturing the name of the User who approves the PO

Is it possible to capture the username who approves or rejects my PO?

A. Yes you can. You can retrieve Actual agent name after workitem execution. It's name is _WI_Actual_Agent. Move it via task parameter binding.

Question 23: BUS2012 user exit not triggering

We have an approval WF for PO(BUS2012). We have the following scenario for a PO:

1. When a PO is created it must trigger an email to respective person for approval of Release;
2. In SWEC i have set up for BUS2012 with 'CREATED' event and Oncreate option is checked;
3. In Task triggering event [standard event], we have Event 'ReleaseStepCreated' is fired;
4. In Task under OBJECT METHOD we have method: 'SINGLERELEASE';
5. In the workflow Template we have 'RELEASESTEPCREATED' as an event;

In release strategy it indicates '9' in the workflow column for Release Code.

We need to use the userexit M06E0005 to use our Purchasing org requirement. However it's not triggerring.

Role is also defined but its not accepting the FM: EXIT_SAPLEBNF_005 which is of userexit M06Er0005.

Any suggestions what could be missing or need to do anything with Role.

A. If you need to connect responsible users to Purchasing group (or even Organizational unit) to evaluate agents in WF, then you can use standard roles (transaction PFAC) with responsibilities. Responsibilities are quite flexible and time dependent.

Question 24: RSWUWFML

Report RSWUWFML and executable attachments

I currently run report RSWUWFML on 4.6C. The work item can be transferred and be seen in Outlook inbox, however, the executable attachment cannot be found. This also happens even for the simple workflow "Approve notification of absence". Why do these problems occur and how can it be resolved?

A. You can use report RSWUWFML2 instead. It's available on 4.6C with basis support package 47 or you can import support section using transport attached to note 691774.

Question 25: Creating Events

Create an Event for New Object Type

I have created a new object type (ZNEW) based on new table that I also recently finished (table ZID). Creating Attributes for my new Object type was simple and I have also managed with the methods. What I would like to do now is to create event 'Created' and 'Changed' to have the following functions:

'Created' - whenever new record is added to table ZID;

'Changed' - whenever record is updated in table ZID;

Are these innovations possible? If so, how can these be done?

A. If your table is being maintained by a custom program, you can call 'SWE_EVENT_CREATE' from the custom program to raise the events 'Created' and Changed' after the record is saved.
If your table is being maintained by a standard DDIC maintenance transaction (i.e. SM30), then you can create a change document (SCDO) function and link the events of your new business object to the change document (SWEC).

Question 26: PO release workflow

I'm using the 'ReleaseStep' created event to trigger my custom PO release workflow . However, this event is triggered even if the release is canceled. How can I configure the system such that my workflow would automatically notify the user (by mail) that it has been cancelled but it still needed to be completed?

A second problem I encountered was with the configuration of the ReleaseStepCreate as the trigger event. When I did this, the ReleaseStepCreate triggers the next work item to the approver. This should not happen automatically. How can I trigger workflow so that PO is created or that only one level is released when necessary? How can I stop the automatic workflow trigger when the release is cancelled?

A. You can handle this before IMM after the WF is triggered and then pass it to your inbox. From there, apply some logic for cancelled release and set the trigger accordingly.

Or:

In the basic data section, start event tab, and then specify conditions.

Question 27: Use position as agent

How do I pass the position to the container from the business object? I have actually copied BUS2013 and want to pass the position from the BOR to WF container. What should be the type of the container? Should the agent be an expression in the activity of the WF?

A. You need to create parameters in BO event and pass position to this. From the event container, you can then map to the workflow container.

Under normal circumstances, you would create an element in the WF and link it to the one in your object. But this would mean that:

1. The element exists in your object as a parameter of the event that will trigger the WF;
2. That before you fire off the event, you populate the parameter of the event with the position;

Question 28: Workflow Substitution

Is there an existing report system or mechanics within the SAP to determine who the approver has substituted with?

To illustrate, an example would be:

PR release task, USER1 is the approver, but USER1 substituted to USER2 for approval.

Is there a report to determine to reflect that USER1 has substituted to USER2?

A. I am not aware of any standard report mechanism availability in SAP. What you do is check with the HRUS_D2. It is the table where you can find the active substitutes for user.

Question 29: Deadline Agents

I am having problems using an expression to identify recipients of a deadline notification. More specifically, the problem occurs only when I utilize a Role as a recipient.

The latest complication I encountered was having the recipient as an expression, of which is also a container element. If I fill that container element with a type "user": like USZTESTID1, it works fine. But, if I fill the container element with a type "role": like AGZTESTROLE1, the recipient does not receive anything

The format of the expression is the first 2 characters representing the "type" of the agent. The rest is the agent itself.

'US = User, AG = Role'

Is this possibly a bug with RSWWDHEX? If so, how can this be resolved?

A. For Rule (AC) and Role (AG) expression cannot be used.
An excerpt from the online documentation:

"You can specify not only a system user, but also a role or an object of Organizational Management such as a position, a Job, an organizational unit or a work center. Alternatively, you can define a container element that contains the object of Organizational Management at runtime or a rule for dynamic agent determination."

Objects of Organizational Management are referred to as "organizational unit, job, position, work center".

Role and Rule are not considered objects of OM.

Question 30: SD, Triggering

I want to trigger my workflow whenever a billing document gets cancelled. For that I wanted to use "VBRK" business object. But "VBRK" doesn't have event "CREATED". It only has an event called "ASSIGNED". So how do I trigger my workflow? Also, what is event "ASSIGNED"?

A. Create a subtype of VBRK and add a new event 'created'. Afterwards, generate and then add this as a system wide delegate for VBRK. You can get this new event to raise (VBRK.Created) through the 'change documents' (SWEC).

Question 31: Display limitation

Is there a way to limit the display to inbox-workflow tasks only?

A. The answer lies in table HRS1201. Check to see if the field 'Background' does not contain an X. If it doesn't then it's a dialog task.

Question 32: Generating index

What is the purpose of button "Refresh index" in screen "Standard task: Maintain Agent Assignment" (in menu Additional data>Agent assignment>Maintain)?

A. Generally, the agents for a task are stored in a cluster (index). The refresh button just populates this cluster. When you push that button, the code function RH_TASK_AGENTS_INDEX is executed.

Question 33: *Priority Problems*

Solving Priority Problems in Workflow

We have 2 different types of workflows. One is for Ordinary Orders and another is for Outage orders. The Ordinary order workflows take 1 minute to complete. Our system is designed so that every morning at 12:00 a.m.,
the deadline monitor job triggers 500 of Ordinary Order Workflows.
We have 15 work process allocated to generate workflows.
It is currently taking 1 minute for each workflow to finish. Hence, it is taking at least 35 minutes to complete all of them. In the mean time, if an Outage Order workflow comes, it has to wait in SM58 queue for 35 minutes before it gets executed. Is there a way to re-program the cycle so that a higher priority is assigned to the Outage order workflows than the Ordinary Order workflows?

A. You can try more connection. Find something in transaction SMOS, parameter max connection.

Question 34: Warning Message

Display a warning message from a background job

We currently have a PR release workflow that is structured as follows:

Step 1. The User gets a workitem in the outlook;
Step 2. While executing the workitem, he sees a Decision step;
Step 3. The User Approves the PR;
Step 4. The PR is released in the background (using std BO2105).

We encounter cases wherein the user approves the PR but the approval does not reach the subsequent level because of an error in the process of releasing. Errors are reflected in the return table.

What we need is for the user to get a warning or error message whenever this happens. How can this be done? Is there a way to pop a message for the user while he is in the same dialog sequence? Generally, Users do not want to go back to Outlook inbox to check for confirmation or error mails as it slows down the work process.

A. You can use TH_POPUP (via a background job) in an old release R/3 (4.6c). For 4.7, you have to use the CALL FUNCTION with the DESTINATION parameter.

For example: if system called 'SAPprd'

Use Code: CALL FUNCTION 'TH_POPUP' DESTINATION 'sapprd_PRD_00'.

This will work in background mode.

Question 35: Debugging Business Object

Is it possible to debug Business Object? Is it also possible to get a trace of the Business Object Event triggers and Method Calls?

A. In TR. SWO1, instantiate the business object. From there you can easily debug methods. To debug a BOR method you just need to put a breakpoint in your method and test the same. You can also debug attributes by placing the breakpoint and then initiating the object. If what you mean by debugging a method for a trigger event – is the method in a task that is triggered by an event, then you will have to debug all the way through the workflow engine from the point where you raised the event (SWUE) until the task calls the method. A breakpoint in one of the binding FMs would be useful here.

To trace the events, switch on the event trace SWELS and view SWEL.

Question 36: PO Release Workflow

Workflow for Purchase order release Procedure

How do you start the configuration for the Purchase order release Procedure?

A. You could start by taking a look at the Std. WF provided by SAP: WS20000075. From there, you would know how to proceed.

Question 37: HR Infotype

Workflow for HR info type

We have the following process for our HR salary loan procedure:

1. The employee requests a loan.
2. The Finance department either approves or rejects.
3. If approved, Finance credits employee account.
4. Afterwards, Finance debits employee salary.

Based on this procedure, our HR consultant has created a special infotype to manage the loan request. The credit/debit is committed via financial invoice.

In addition, we wish to integrate these operations via workflow. My problem is there is no standard business object (!). Creating the HR infotype also generates business object concerns. How do I work around special issues concerning the creation of the business object?

A. The standard Business Objects for infotypes is BUS1065, EMPLOYEET, (PFBASIC). The Event linkage can be done in SWEHR3. In here, you can link workflows to different infotype operations via PA30.

Question 38: Workflow for material creation

I have to setup workflow for material creation. Whenever a new material is created by engineering, I have to design a workflow so that every other department can maintain the views. The requirement is that there should be flow and notification by email between departments for maintaining all the views of material master. How do I proceed to do this?

A. You may follow these steps to start with:

1) Create change documents for tables of material in material master - transaction SCDO;
2) Then, create your own business object, please note the key field; it must coincide with key fields of tables of material in material master - transaction SWO1;
3) Afterwards, create event "CHANGE" for your BO from point 2 and for your change document from point 1 - transaction SWU_EWCD;
4) Finally, create your WF start of triggering event from point 3.

Question 39: Transport of General Task

I've got a problem with the agent assignment. During the development process, I'm either setting the task as General task or I'm assigning it to an Org structure.

Previously, there hasn't been any problem. But for some reason, when I'm transporting it now, there isn't any agent assignment in any of the systems I'm transferring it to.

I found one SAP-note (72715) on it, but it was from 2001, and for versions 3.0A-3.1G, promising that it would be OK from 3.1H. Currently we're on version 4.7.

What I know is that since the last time I put up a WF we have started implementing CRM and also starting to use the HR functionality. I've checked, and none in these projects have knowingly made any changes. Is there any way to resolve this?

A. Go to transaction OOCR and clear the field Value Abbr. for line TRSP CORR.
Then you can create a transport request for making a task general.

Question 40: Workflow Performance

In my scenario, a particular WF is going to be triggered after data migration of approx. 100000 records. i.e. around those many instances will be created.

My question is, should I anticipate a performance issue? Shall we go for Event queue in this case?

If we go for event queue administration, we need inputs on the following points:

1. Whether should we select linkage type as – Mark linkage as having errors?

2. Inputs for parameters for Background job scheduling:

In respect of – Number of events to be read (considering case of 100000 records) and time interval.

Another factor to consider is if we can mention event delivery sequential and asyn. mode, for this case?

A. For your requirements, you can use transaction SMQS and SWEQADM.

If there is more work item, then activation of event queue is always advisable. Keep in mind how many work processes you are assigning for event queue.

Question 41: PR Approval

Notification by email after PR has been completely approved

I have workflow in use for PR release strategy. The requirement is after all agents involved have approved the PR, in other words PR is released for PO and emails should be sent to those agents. I tried to use the event 'Released' (BO BUS2105), but this event is triggered every time PR Release code is approved. How can I fix this?

A. You need to add one step which will be based on release strategy. Necessarily, corresponding method will be in your BUS2105 object type, I am guessing ZBUS2105 or whatever you have already created. It will check the key field of bus2105 that is PR, directly go to table and check the release strategy codes. See if you can use related transparent tables r t1 6FS and t16fc.

This requires a bit of abap work but from here, you can maintain the person(s) to whom you want to send email.

Question 42: Purchasing Workflows

Standard workflow in Purchase requisition and Purchase order

What are the required settings to be done for activating the standard workflow in purchase order and purchase requisition?

I tried the setting up one for the organizational plan, but it is not throwing the messages to the user in his SAP inbox. What could be the conflict here and how could this be resolved?

A. Do workflow configuration by just running the transaction. Then, create organization in workflow/HR area. From there copy std workflow WS20000075 to a customized workflow. Make changes as required. Set the triggering event. It should work smoothly afterwards.

Question 43: Approval for new cost center

I have a requirement for approving new cost centers .When the user creates
cost center, I have to send approval for n level. Is there any standard cost center approval workflow?

A. There is no SAP standard cost center approval workflow. Workflow can only automate an existing process or a process you are about to develop. One option would be to design a process where you store the data in a Z table, get the approvals and then create the CC.

Question 44: Workflow for IDOC Error

What are the configurations or steps needed for the IDOC error notification workflows to work?

A. Go to the IDOC configuration. Set the "Business object" and event to be used. From there, you can define the agents who were receiving the message in IDOC configuration. Then, search from the corresponding standard task in PFTC. Lastly, activate the event linkage in task.

Question 45: Release Strategies

SAP standard workflow for release strategies

I need to implement the SAP standard workflow for release strategies for PR. I have done all the customization required for release strategies, maintained release codes as workflow relevant, and assigned Agent ID to release codes. Now to use the SAP standard workflow for release strategies is it possible to just use workflow template 40000001 (WWW scenario: release of purchase requirement)? What are the steps that I need to perform to use this template for my workflow?

A. You just need to link the workflow template to BUS2012. Afterwards, RELEASESTEPCREATED in SWE2, and then test it.

As you are using standard template in SWDD_CONFIG transaction, you can change the workitem descriptions in accordance to the requirements.
If there are any user decision steps to make, you need to define agents.
You may also need to activate the event linkage. From here, everything should work fine.

Question 46: Error Status

Possibility to complete a workflow with an 'ERROR' status

The workflow I'm supporting has a wait event that is supposed to be completed if a new workflow is started for the same FIPP document. The problem is that if the original workflow errors and then a new workflow is triggered for the same document, then the original workflow is not completed. It stays in 'ERROR' status. Meanwhile, the graphical workflow log shows that the wait step has been triggered.

Is it possible that a workflow in error could still be completed or is it only possible for a workflow that is in 'In-Process' state?

A. You can try to enter the work item in change mode. Press 'Restart after error' and then 'Complete manually'.

Or another option would be logically deleting the work item.

Do this by going to display task-->menu option--> technical work item display→edit--> change. From hereon, you will find the button→ delete logically. Your work flow will then be completed.

As another workflow is in process for the same document, you can delete workitem logically. That will not affect the new workflow that is in process. If the workflow is going to reflect 'error' every time a new WF starts for the same document, you may need to handle error in workflow.

Question 47: List all Workflows

What is the transaction code for listing all the workflows in the system (including standard & customized workflows)?

A. Use se16 and table name 'HRSOOBJECT'. It will list all the workflows. It also lists Roles but you can restrict by selecting TS, TG and WS.

Or another option is to use the transaction SWE2/SWETYPV, and check the active type linkage.

SAP Business Workflow Interview Questions

Question 48: SWUS transaction workflow

What are the relevant details of SWUS transaction workflow? What is the difference between the 'Execute' and 'Execute with debugging on mode'? Why is it that if a task works fine using the 'Execute with debugging mode', it doesn't work at all if I use the 'Execute' mode only?

A. The SWUS SAP transaction is utilized to test the workflow. If you have created the workflow template in wbuilder, then you can test it as well. Pass the data in 'input' push button. If you want to check that whether any workflow has started or not, you can check with the log.

If your workflow template is not working as expected, you can diagnose it using transaction SWUD. Supply the WS and 8 digit name of your task appropriately.

Question 49: Terminating Events

Problems defining a terminating event

I have a requirement that if the PR is changed during the PR release then the workflow does not need to start. The problem is my workflow is triggering on the event 'RELEASESTEPCREATED' for Bus2105. This event is also triggered with 'CHANGEDSIGNIFICANTLY' event, when someone changes the value of the PR. The workflow is triggered as well. I tried to configure the start-condition as well as define a wait-event step. However, both do not work and the workflow continues to trigger.

How can this be resolved to fulfill the requirement?

A. In type linkage you can attach your own Check Function module. In check function module you can define your own conditions when to pass this event to the receiver (in your WF template). Try to put the conditions in Check function module.
You can also possibly redefine your release strategy with the help of MM guy, in PR classifications. The price is also a criterion to determine the release strategy. This is dependent on how you would you like to go. Check fn. Module. It is one of the best solutions.

Question 50: Send email when invoice is posted

How could I create a simple workflow to let the system post an invoice for a specific customer? Is it possible to send an email only in that situation: Customer (10025)?

A. You have two ways to send mail. One is to use user-exit or BAdI to send mail using transaction commit. Two is to check a customer data in WF. Look for BUS2081-->event: assigned→ created→ posted→ blockedPrice→ blockedQuant→ released→ cancelled→ parked→ completed→ approved→ →deleted→completedChanged→completedToRelease .

To ensure that it only fires for a specific customer, your best bet is to use start conditions looking for LIFNR = 10025.

Question 51: WF queries

Why is it that my workflow is intermittently sending two emails for verification on the leave application WF?

A. The function of receiving mails is dependent on your WF definition. Re-check the WF definition.

Question 52: SWDD configuration

What is the difference between SWDD and SWDD configuration?

A. SWDD_CONFIG is used to make changes to SAP WF templates. This transaction allows you to make changes like workitem texts, agents and step names. On the other hand, SWDD is used to create your own WF templates.

Question 53: Triggering Events

ReleaseStepCreated did not trigger BUS2013/BUS2014

We have approval WF for PO(BUS2012),SA(BUS2013) and Contracts(BUS2013). We also have the following scenario for a PO:

1. When a PO is changed (Value/new line item) and its approval is still in process a 'Blocked state' event 'CHANGED' is fired;
2. When a PO is changed when it is in a Release state, event 'ReleaseStepCreated' is fired along with 'CHANGED';

This is not materializing for SA and Contracts. I checked the release strategy for them and found all of them had '9' in the workflow column for Release Code.

Any suggestions what could be missing?

More recently, I had to change the workflows for PO/SA/Contracts.

Changes made were as follows:

1. WF templates;
2. Created a custom task with logic;

3. Created FM;
4. Created a custom object for the method in 2;

During testing, the following were observed:

1. When we change an SA/Contract, ME32L and
ME33K do not reset the release back in blocked
status. This is why event ReleaseStepCreated is not
triggered. I checked with the functional team and they
said nothing changed in release strategy.
2. I checked in our quality s   ystem and found
that ME32L and ME33K work fine during changes.
3. Assuming that my development is independent of
these transactions, transport was moved to Quality
system.
4. Unfortunately, ME32L and ME33K started
behaving in same manner as in development box.

Confusion was caused by the facts that:
1. There was no move in the customization;
2. There was no change and movement in the
BUS2013 and BUS2014;
3. Even the standard transactions were not moved
(assuming some change due to application of SAP
patches);

My question is, what could we have missed during
configuration and troubleshooting? Why is the
ReleaseStepCreated not triggering
BUS2013/BUS2014?

A. The release strategy with '9' in Workflow points to User Execute EXIT_SAPLEBNF_005.

You can check two things to determine what is wrong. Do the following:

1. Check design of EXIT_SAPLEBNF_005, it is not able to return any WF Agents.
2. Check SM58 to get an error listing of RFC workflow error calls.

From hereon, you will know for sure where the conflict started.

Question 54: Triggering events

Triggering BUS2105.significantlychanged

Which changes in a purchase requisition would be considered applicable to Workflow?

A. These would be the changes that lead to a new Release group or Release strategy.

Question 55: Pop-ups for workflow

Is it possible to configure the SAP workflow to have a pop-up message sent to the approver in the instance that Purchase Requisitions are ready for them to act on?

A. You can either send an Express Email message, or if it is a workitem, then make the Priority = 9. It will send an express message to the Respective Agent.

Question 56: Replace the user in workflow

I have a requirement to have User A be replaced with User B in a workflow. No other details were given for the required task except that user A is no longer with the organization. How can I configure this into the existing set-up?

A. Go to that particular IDOC configuration (t-code WE20) and find the agents attached there. If the agent is determined through user id you can change the user id to B. If it is maintained using work center you need to update the work center in accordance to your requirements.

Question 57: Resubmitted WI

Resubmitted WI doesn't get triggered

I discovered that there are some work items that were put for re-submission until Oct 1st 2005 that haven't been returned to the inbox yet. The log indicates status 'waiting'. I checked SWU3 and everything seems to be working fine. I also checked all of our batch jobs in the system that is supposed to take care of these programs:

RSWWDHEX
RSWWCLEAR
RSWWCOND
RSWWDHEX
RSWWERRE

Everything seems to be running smoothly.

I can't find anything wrong in the documentation. Where is the bottleneck coming from? Why is the re-submitted work not coming in the inbox automatically?

A. First, I would recommend you to search through previous operational notes if this had happened before. Second, write an OSS and let SAP sort it out. If it's nothing else in operations then it's their functionality that's not working.

Question 58: Workflow without HR

Workflow implementation without HR

Our client is planning to implement a few FI and MM workflow as part of the Release 1 implementation. They will not have HR in SAP at that time (HR will be in Release 2 implementation).

Can you please let me know how we can implement Workflow - Agent Assignment, User Identification etc. without HR? If we need to do approval then will we need approval hierarchy?

A. Part of HR necessary for WF may be used without implementation HR.
In transaction PPOM, you may assign Agents with assigned Users as is necessary in support of WF. You still can define an Org Hierarchy without HR, define organization structure, jobs, positions, and every other needed object.

Your second option is to define roles and use those roles in the agent assignment. Roles can be based on the custom function module also.

A third option will be to build a custom table to hold the agent information. Then create custom FMs tied to a RULE which would query the table and, based on the information in the workflow containers, determine which agent(s) to route the work item to.

If you go this route, consider creating a custom transaction and give the users a custom screen (and not sm30) to maintain the table. Our screen looked like a hierarchy so they used the drop-down to select the agents. Using this, they could visually see to whom and in what order the work items would be routed.

Question 59: Business workplace Inbox clean up

I'd just like to know if there's a way for the basis admin to delete unwanted/old mails in the business workplace. Is there an abap program which I can schedule once a month?

A. Transaction SWWL (program RSWWWIDE) will delete workitems periodically but you need to be extremely careful running it in a productive environment. This is because you may end up unnecessarily deleting items that you did not want to. You should also run SWWH (program RSWWHIDE) to delete the workitem history for those workitems. This is an extreme operation though.

I would strongly recommend using an archive instead. Archive out your completed workitems via SARA, object WORKITEM. This way, you can retrieve files whenever necessary.

Question 60: Items to WF-BATCH

Released items go to WF-BATCH inbox instead of WF_Initiator

I created a new workflow and inserted standard workflow WS20000077 inside (so I can add additional custom steps later). It worked fine until Purchase Requirement was released. The next step should have been to send notification to WF_Initiator. However, instead of going to the initiator/agent, items go to WF-Batch's inbox (with status of READY).

The interesting thing is that if I deactivate my workflow and activate WS20000077 all by itself it works fine (user who initiated workflow gets a message stating requirement was released). I have the exact same steps and tasks in my workflow, and the same settings. Why is it then that the items go to WF-Batch and not the initiator/agent?

A. This appears to be a binding issue. Check and make sure that you bind the initiator from your custom workflow to your sub-workflow.
You may also need to go to the activity step where you've defined the subworkflow, then check the workflow to task bindings. There should be a blank entry for the workflow initiator, which you can just bind to the actual agent in your workflow container.

If you can't see this entry (and I think this is why you couldn't find it), just expand the list of possible bindings with the green down arrow button.

Question 61: Setting Dialogue tasks

How can I set the foreground/dialogue tasks to "general tasks"?

A. Go to Task--> additional data-->agents-->maintain agents screen→click on properties. In there, you will get a pop-up, then select "general task".

Question 62: Workflow problem

I use the User decision activity as one of the step of workflow. This works properly but after the step in workflow, I use condition activity. This would reflect the condition as always false. But if I check the value in the container, the value is true. What could be the problem in the workflow?

A. This is either a binding or buffering problem. Check the definition of your container elements correctly and proceed from there.

Question 63: Spool Failure

Sending a message to user inbox on spool failure

When we create a Purchase order and print the same or send it via mail, a spool is created. In case the spool fails, a message should be sent to the user who created the spool. How can this be configured?

A. The first thing to do is to check whether it's possible to trigger a workflow based on a spool failure. To do this, check the event log after a spool failure occurs (SWEL - make sure it's switched on!) to see whether anything is raised for your test case.

If you do have an event, you're pretty much there - you can just create a very simple one-step workflow based around a notification mail (something using SELFITEM or STD_TEXT should do it).

If this does not work, there is another approach that could be taken. Do the following steps:

1) Check OSS notes to see whether there's any configuration you need to do to get your event to rise - you might even put in a query yourself. Often that's the only way to get a true answer to this sort of problem;

If you draw a blank, then try the following:

2) See whether there's a user exit that gets called if the spool fails - if so, you could raise your event programmatically using 'SWE_EVENT_CREATE'.

3) If that fails, you could look at writing an ABAP report to raise your event based on it detecting that a spool has failed (perhaps through querying new entries in the underlying SAP table), then set that ABAP to run as a scheduled job.

Question 64: Substitution Questions

1) We would like to trace which user had maintained its workflow substitution in SBWP -> settings -> workflow settings -> maintain/activate substitute. We had already activated the audit log SM19/SM20, however the audit trail only reflected the respective user had logon to SBWP etc. It did not log further detail what he had done in SBWP. Is there any other table or tools that we can utilize to see those detailed info?

2) Are there any transactions/reports/tables we can list at present which users had set/activated his workflow substitution in SBWP?

3) If we remove the authorization for the workflow substitution in SBWP, what authorization object can be modified?

4) Is there any central transaction that we can use to maintain ALL user workflow substitution that they can maintain themselves so we can use SO36 to centrally maintain the auto-forwarding for all user IDs?

5) How do you determine active and passive substitutes?

A. First, take a look at table HRUS_D2. From there, you can create a maintenance view for this to allow mass maintenance of substitutes.

Secondly, there is an FM to maintain users' substitutions:

'SWL_SUBSTITUTION_DEFINE'

Here's a little ABAP I've found on the net to call the FM:

```
*----------------------------------------------------------------*
* Program: Z_DEFINE_SUBSTITUTE *
* Author: Erik Gouw, Avelon *
*----------------------------------------------------------------*
SELECTION-SCREEN BEGIN OF BLOCK selection
WITH FRAME.
PARAMETERS: p_user type uname matchcode object
USER_ADDR.
SELECTION-SCREEN END OF BLOCK selection.
CALL FUNCTION 'SWL_SUBSTITUTION_DEFINE'
EXPORTING
User = p_user.
```

Lastly, look at table HRUS_D2. The 'ACTIVE' field will tell you whether the substitution is active or passive.

Question 65: Condition Step

Defining Condition Step in a Workflow

How do you define a condition step? In an expression, I am checking the WF container element value. For TRUE value, I want to continue to the next step, and for FALSE I want to exit workflow, as this "next step" is the last step in a WF. However, when I come back to WF Builder, I can see that both results bring me to the "next step". What I am missing here to correctly configure the TRUE and FALSE values?

A. You need to add a process control step to complete the workflow in false branch.

Question 66: Virtual Attribute

I have a virtual attribute 'UserName' in my own business object. During the test, BO works fine. But when I used this virtual attribute in the task WF and used transaction SWUS, that value from virtual attribute was null.
In the code of my BO I read:

GET_PROPERTY UserName CHANGING CONTAINER.

Data: wa_adrp type adrp.

Select single f~NAME_TEXT
Into corresponding fields of wa_adrp
From adrp as f inner join usr21 as p
On f~PERSNUMBER = p~PERSNUMBER
Where p~BNAME = kod.

OBJECT-UserName = wa_adrp-NAME_TEXT.
SWC_SET_ELEMENT CONTAINER 'UserName'
OBJECT-UserName.

END_PROPERTY.

Status of virtual attribute is 'implemented' and BO is fully generated.

What can be the problem here? How can this be resolved?

A. If the status of the business object is "Implemented", then this is not consistent. Please change the status to "Released" and try again.

Question 67: *Role container value*

Please help me out, how do I take Role Container Actor Tab values into work flow container element?

A. You should check the binding. Normal binding of container element from WF to task should accomplish this.

In terms of a task to workflow binding, you'd typically only want to pass back actual agent back into your workflow. There's no real linkage between a role container and the workflow container, unless you've created an extra step in your workflow/a virtual attribute to evaluate a role and pass the results to a workflow container element so you can set your agent assignment for a subsequent workflow step via an expression.

Question 68: Audit Trace

We are testing FI Document Parking Workflow Object FIPP in 4.7.

When the document is posted by the last approver, we can see that the document is posted or entered by: WF-BATCH.

Is it possible to get the last approver's name in the Parked by field? Or else,
how can we show the audit trace or log of the document was approved by the right person?

A. One trick is to change the properties of whichever method you're using to post the document so that it's synchronous/dialog. Then check the 'advance with dialog' box on the task configuration screen to form a processing chain.

This means that whenever your user makes the final approval, the posting action will kick in straight away and the document will be posted under his/her ID.

Rather than changing the standard SAP business object, it's always best to create your own subtype, than to delegate that system-wide to the super type via SWO6.

Question 69: Starting Workflow

Raise ABAP Class event to start workflow

I am working on R/3 version 4.7 (Basis 6.4). In here, I have noticed that you can specify event linkages - either a BO event or a CL event.

I created my class with a static event. The class inherits from IF_WORKLFLOW, so that it can be used in workflows. In the workflow, I have specified to use CL events, and I have specified my class and event. I have then set up all binding and everything activates fine.

From there, I created a static method in my class to raise the event. I have a small ABAP which calls the static method, which in turn, raises the static event. From my understanding, the workflow should then be triggered, because my event was raised.

The event linkage is active but that doesn't work. So I went to test it in transaction SWU0. I specified my object category as ABAP Class, object type is my "Z" class, which I can select from the F4 help, and same with the event.
I execute, and it tells me that everything is working fine. All the tasks that should be started are shown, and no errors or warnings exist. My question is, why doesn't it trigger the event correctly? How can I correct this situation?

A. The issue has more to do between the linkage between the event and your workflow. Check out that SWE2 has been set-up correctly, and see if you can clearly see a mapping between your event and your workflow, and that it should be enabled.

You can also check the event queue if it is enabled (check SWEQADM). While doing that, check to see whether the event is being delivered there instead...

If the problem still persists after the above solutions, try raising the event via SWUE. If this still doesn't work, the next step would actually be to debug the standard SAP code when you raise your event to see where it's going wrong. From there, a more detailed configuration solution can be mapped out.

Question 70: Material Change Workflow

How can I configure workflow to track record for every change of material in material master?

A. Do the following steps:

1) Create change documents for tables of material in material master - transaction SCDO.
2) Create your own business object, please note key field - it must coincide
With key fields of tables of material in material master, transaction SWO1.
3) Create event "CHANGE" for your BO from point 2 and for your change document from point 1 - transaction SWU_EWCD.
4) Create your WF start of triggering event from point 3.

Question 71: Resend Workflow

Resend workflow to another agent

Workflow was sent to an agent but the agent is out of office. I need to send the workflow to another agent but I do not know how. Do I have to retrigger the workflow? If not, what are my options for re-configuration?

A. You may use transaction SWIA to execute WF without agent check. If this task has agents "Role", it is possible to use transaction ppom for assigning the Role Users. After which you can now use transaction ppwfbuf.

Question 72: Email Notification

We have a problem in sending formatted mail. We are currently using 'SO_NEW_DOCUMENT_ATT_SEND_API1' function module to pass the email content. This function module formats everything in plain text. However, our requirement is to send mail with some part of the text in a specific font and color with underlines. How do I reformat the function module with these requirements?

A. Check out report RSWUWFMLEC. This is used to send emails in text or HTML format.

It also uses SO_NEW_DOCUMENT_ATT_SEND_API1, but this function is becoming obsolete. For example, it truncates the mail subject beyond the 50th character. There is an OSS note which solves this by replacing the call to this function module with an object-oriented approach.

Another approach that you might want to try is to find in your workflow 'created Tasks'→Workflow Builder→Send mail Select→TAB Requested END. Then, check the "Text to be Requested" → Go inside and you can write any mail text format there.

Question 73: Error Handing

I need to create an error handling workflow to call a screen transaction. To do this, I need to create a Business Object with a method that calls this transaction.

My question is, how do I pass the data into the transaction so that it is processed? Normally this is done with the 'CALL TRANSACTION' command and pass the data via a BDC table. I have analyzed the IDOC_INPUT_ORDERS function module extensively, and have seen that a BDC table is created from the data in the IDOC.

The workflow task will have data mapped from the IDOC into the container for the task. Do I also need to explicitly map the data in the container of the workflow item to a BDC session before processing?

A. The trick I here is to pass the values to your custom transaction via the ABAP/4 memory.

In your method code, use the 'export to memory' ID ABAP commands to store the variables. Then call your transaction.

In your 'Process Before Output' script, just add an extra form which imports the variables and put them in the right place. Remember to clear them once they've been retrieved.

Of course, that's for custom transactions. If it's a standard SAP screen, then your options are:
1) Find a BAPI or function module that you can call from your method instead - 'BAPI_SALESORDER_CREATE' if it's a sales order;
2) Create a BDC table and do call transaction as you've already suggested.

Question 74: *Distribution Lists*

Assigning SAP Office Distribution List in Workflow Task

How do I assign a distribution list instead of an org-object in workflow task?
We have a group of engineers and managers who do not have SAP log-on since the group monitoring output of this workflow is dynamic and are not part of the formal organizational structure.

Does it mean that creating a dummy organizational structure will also entail updating positions and transporting it every time?

A. You can use the rule ac30000012 and hard code the SAP distribution list. Make sure it is a shared type format.

Question 75: Work item execution

Work item not getting executed

I encountered a problem while trying to execute a work item in the receiver's inbox. I'm putting the notification through ESS by generating web transactions. The notification is going to the inbox. However, it is showing an error while executing the item:

"Work item 000000021121: Object method SWW_WW_EXECUTE_S cannot be executed".

How can this be resolved?

A. Check your authorization to the transaction that is being executed.

Question 76: Work Item and Notification

What differences are there between a work item and a notification mail?

A. The work item cannot be used to notify several users. Mails can be routed to several users, just like work items. When a mail is sent, and one recipient reads and deletes the mail, all other recipients will still have access to their own copy in their own inbox. However, when a work item is processed by one of the recipients it will automatically disappear from all the other inboxes. So you can see that a work item is unsuitable for notifying several users. It is also worth noting that a mail can be forwarded in many different ways (fax, internet...) whereas the work item cannot.

b) The work item holds up the workflow
When the workflow sends a mail (usually as a background step) it continues with the process immediately after transmitting the mail. When a work item is generated, the workflow will not continue until the work item has been processed. This slows down the process. Occasionally this is what is intended (using the work item as an approval step without the ability to reject) but
usually you will better off using mails for notifications.

Note: You can send business objects as references with the mail either as a business object reference attached to the mail or as an URL (ABAP required).

Question 77: *Email Recipients*

What is the difference between sending a mail to a recipient list compared to sending individual mails via a dynamic loop?

A. Performance. Sending 1 mail to 20 recipients will cost considerably less performance than sending 20 individual mails. If the mail is sent as a SAP Office mail (as opposed to e-mail, fax...) disk space will also be a factor because the SAP office mail will only exist once in the database, with references being created for each of the recipients.

The only time you need to consider individual mails with a dynamic loop is when the text of the mail varies from one recipient to another.

Question 78: Sending Text

How do I send a standard text as an e-mail from workflow?

It is very easy sending standard text , which may include data from the workflow. You simply create a background step which sends the work item description. This may include variables which will be substituted when mail is sent.

In early releases you have to create your own task based on the method SELFITEM SendTaskDescription. In later releases a wizard is available for creating the step and in release 4.6 there is even a step type which does this all for you automatically.
Whichever path you take, there is very good online documentation describing exactly what has to be done.

Question 79: Complex Text

How do I send a complex text from the workflow?

A. You may create mails using SAPscript. These mails can include conditions which are evaluated in order to determine which text blocks which are used in the mail. Workflow variables can be used in these conditions and workflow variables can be substituted into the body of the e-mail text.

Question 80: Really Complex Email

How do I send really complex mails from the workflow?

If you this is not enough for you will probably want to write your own ABAP routines for generating the text and generating the attachments to go with the text.

Use the function group SO01 which contains functions of the form SO_*_API1 which are ideal for creating your own sophisticated messages. There are plenty of advantages of how these are used within the SAP system.

Question 81: How do I send reports?

A. There are wizards (Release 3.1) which will create workflows for you to send reports to a distribution list. You can specify whether the results should be transmitted or evaluated at the time the recipient wishes to view the report. It is usually better to send the evaluation because this allows the recipient to see the results instantaneously, without having to wait for the
report to execute first.

Question 82: Different Emails

How can I configure the workflow so that different types of messages are sent out to different people depending on how late the processing is?

A. Follow these steps:

1. Specify a deadline period for the step.
2. Specify a name for the event. This adds new branch from the step. More...
3. Add a new step to the branch which sends a mail message.
4. Add another step to the branch which sends out the second deadline warning (see mail steps above). Use deadlines in this step to configure an earliest start so that the second message is not sent until a further time has elapsed.
5. Repeat step 5 as often as you like.

Question 83: Deadline Step Missed

How can I configure the workflow so that when the deadline is missed the workflow step is simply skipped?

A. This is tricky to explain but easy to implement once you know how.
Follow these steps (in later releases there is a wizard which takes you through the steps):
1. In the terminating events view of the workflow step activate the "obsolete" event and give it a name. More...
2. Specify a deadline period for the step.
3. Specify a name for the event. This adds new branch from the step. More...
4. Add a new step to the deadline path. This step must be of type "process control".
5. Select the control "Make step obsolete" and use the search help to specify the workflow step that has the deadline. Only steps with obsolete paths defined will be displayed (see step 1).

Question 84: Workflow triggers Email

How do I trigger a workflow with an e-mail?

A. You can customize the system to call a BOR method when an external mail (fax, e-mail...) arrives in the system. You BOR method should either trigger the e-meil directly or trigger an event. To customize this user exit use the transaction SCOT.

Question 85: Accessing Tasks

How can I make sure that user's access their tasks via the workflow and not via the menu or launch pad?

A. The routing mechanism for work items uses roles and organizational assignments to determine who receives which work item. However the routing does not provide extra authorization checks based on the routing configuration. If you want to ensure that the tasks are executed within the workflow, and not via the standard transaction, service or MiniApp, then you will have to apply your own protection.
The simplest way of doing this is to remove the standard transaction from the user's menu or Workplace role (but include it in the supervisor's role, just in case).

If you want to allow the user to execute the task from the menu if and only if they have received the work item then you should replace the standard transaction with your own custom built transaction. Your own transaction simply calls the standard transaction but performs it's own authorization check first, based on the routing mechanism used in the workflow.
Tip: Add a second (ored) authorization check to make sure that a supervisor can execute the transaction in an emergency.

Question 86: Deadline Step

How do you create a new branch for a deadline step?

A. By specifying the event name for a missed deadline (of whatever type) you are indirectly telling the workflow system that you want to add flow logic to your workflow to meet this event.
Don't be put off by he fact that the branch does not lead anywhere. This is because the branch is not an alternative to the other results of the step. It is followed in addition to the other paths. In other words the workflow processing specified for a missed deadline is followed without affecting the standard flow. The step with the missed deadline remains where it is and can still
be processed as normal

Part II: Table & Transaction Code Reference

Important OSS Notes

322526	Debugging workflows
217229	Accessing the Consultants forum for SAP Business Workflow/WebFlow
152871	Release Upgrade considerations for workflow
134322	New Workflow Academy - Course TAWF10
131795	Automatic e-mail notifications
125400	Modifying a productive Workflow
72923	Workflow interfaces
72923	Business Workflow Performance

Transaction Code Reference

AWUV Wizard for event creation *Definition tools –> Event creation –> Set up with wizard*
- **MCA1** Workflow Information System *Reporting –> Workflow Information System (WIS)*
- **OOAW** Evaluation paths
- **PFAC** Maintain standard roles
- **PFAC_CHG** Change roles *Definition tools –> Standard roles –> Change*
- **PFAC_DEL** Delete roles *Definition tools –> Standard roles –> Delete*
- **PFAC_DIS** Display roles *Definition tools –> Standard roles –> Display*
- **PFAC_INS** Create roles *Definition tools –> Standard roles –> Create*
- **PFOM** Maintain assignment to SAP organizational objects *Definition tools –> SAP org. objects –> Create assignments*
- **PFOS** Display assignment to SAP organizational objects *Definition tools –> SAP org. objects –> Display assignments*
- **PFSO** Organizational environment of a user
- **PFT** Maintain customer task
- **PFTC** General task maintenance
- **PFTC_CHG** Change tasks *Definition tools –> Task/Task groups –> Change*
- **PFTC_COP** Copy tasks *Definition tools –> Task/Task groups –> Copy*

- **PFTC_DEL** Delete tasks *Definition tools –> Task/Task groups –> Delete*
- **PFTC_DIS** Display tasks *Definition tools –> Task/Task groups –> Display*
- **PFTC_INS** Create tasks *Definition tools –> Task/Task groups –> Create*
- **PFTR** Standard task for transaction
- **PFTS** Standard task
- **PFWF** Maintain workflow task (customer)
- **PFWS** Maintain workflow template
- **PPOC** Create organizational plan *Definition tools –> Organizational plan –> Create*
- **PPOM** Maintain organizational plan *Definition tools –> Organizational plan –> Change*
- **PPOS** Display organizational plan *Definition tools –> Organizational plan –> Display*
- **SWDA** Ongoing Settings *Administration –> Settings*
- **SWDC** Workflow editor administration data
- **SWDM** Business Workflow Explorer *Definition tools –> Business Workflow Explorer*
- **SWE2** Display and maintain event type linkage *Utilities –> Events –> Type linkages*
- **SWE3** Display instance linkages *Utilities –> Events –> Instance linkages*
- **SWE4** Switch event log on/off *Utilities –> Events –> Event/log –> On/Off*

- **SWEC**   Link change documents to events
  *Definition tools –> Event creation –> Change
  documents –> Linkage*
- **SWED**   Assignment of change document
  objects to object types   *Definition tools –>
  Event creation –> Change documents –>
  Define workflow properties*
- **SWEL**   Display event log   *Utilities –> Events
  –> Event log –> Display*
- **SWF3**   Workflow Wizard Explorer
  *Definition tools –> Wizards –> Workflow
  Wizard Explorer*
- **SWF4**   Workflow Wizard Repository
  *Definition tools –> Wizards –> Workflow
  Wizard Repository*
- **SWI1**   Selection report for workflows
  Utilities –> Work item selection
- **SWI2**   Work item analysis   *Reporting –>
  Work item analysis*
- **SWI3**   Workflow outbox   *Runtime tools –>
  Workflow outbox*
- **SWI4**   Task analysis   *Reporting –> Task
  analysis*
- **SWI5**   Workload analysis   *Reporting –>
  Workload analysis*
- **SWI6**   Object links   *Runtime tools –> Object
  links*
- **SWI7**   Workflow resubmission folder   From
  Integrated Inbox or Workflow Outbox
- **SWI8**   Error overview   Part of
  administration of workflow runtime system
  (transaction SWUF)

- **SWL1**   Settings for dynamic columns Customizing, part of ongoing settings
- **SWLC**   Check tasks for agents   *Utilities –> Consistency check –> Organizational assignment*
- **SWLD**   Workbench for Workflow 4.0
- **SWLP**   Copy plan version
- **SWLV**   Maintain work item views Customizing, part of ongoing settingS
- **SWLW**   Workbench for Workflow 3.0
- **SWO1**   Business Object Builder   *Definition tools –> Business Object Builder*
- **SWO6**   Customizing object types   *From Business Object Builder, choose Settings –> Delegate –> System-wide*
- **SWUO**   Event simulation   *Utilities –> Events –> Simulate event*
- **SWU2**   RFC monitor   *Utilities –> Workflow RFC monitor*
- **SWU3**   Customizing consistency check *Utilities –> Customizing*
- **SWU4**   Consistency check for standard tasks   *Utilities –> Consistency check –> Task –> Standard task*
- **SWU5**   Consistency check for customer tasks   *Utilities –> Consistency check –> Task –> Customer task*
- **SWU6**   Consistency check for workflow tasks   *Utilities –> Consistency check –> Task –> Workflow task*

- **SWU7** Consistency check for workflow templates *Utilities –> Consistency check –> Task –> Workflow template*
- **SWU8** Switch technical trace on/off *Utilities –> Technical trace –> On/off*
- **SWU9** Display technical trace *Utilities –> Technical trace –> Display*
- **SWUD** Diagnostic tools *Utilities –> Diagnosis*
- **SWUE** Trigger event *Utilities –> Events –> Generate event*
- **SWUF** Runtime system administration *Administration –> Runtime system*
- **SWUG** Workflow start transactions *Definition tools –> Workflow start transactions*
- **SWUI** Start workflows From the R/3 initial screen, choose *Office –> Start Workflow*
- **SWUS** Start tasks *Runtime tools –> Start workflow*
- **SWUY** Wizard for message linkage to workflow *Definition tools –> Wizards –> Create "Call workflow from message"*
- **SWX1** Create notification of absence
- **SWX2** Change notification of absence
- **SWX3** Display notification of absence
- **SWX4** Approve notification of absence
- **SWXF** Form applications: Access point *Environment –> Demo examples –> Fill out form*

Reports

- **RSWWWIDE** – Delete work items
- **RHSOBJCH** to fix PD Control Tables

Tables
- **SWW_OUTBOX** - Lists Workflows in outbox together with status
- **SWW_CONT** - Container Contents for Work Item Data Container
- **SWW_CONTOB** - Container Cont. for Work Item Data Container (Only Objects)
- **SWWLOGHIST** - History of a work item
- **SWWORGTASK** - Assignment of WIs to Org.Units and Tasks
- **SWWUSERWI** - Current Work Items Assigned to a User
- **SWWWIHEAD** - Header Table for all Work Item Types

INDEX

SAP Business Workflow Interview Questions

Attention SAP Experts

Writing a book can be the best thing for your career.

Have you ever considered writing a book in your area of SAP? Equity Press is the leading provider of knowledge products in SAP applications consulting, development, and support. If you have a manuscript or an idea of a manuscript, we'd love to help you get it published!

Please send your manuscript or manuscript ideas to **jim@sapcookbook.com** – we'll help you turn your dream into a reality.

Or mail your inquiries to:

Equity Press Manuscripts
BOX 706
Riverside, California
92502

Tel (951)788-0810
Fax (951)788-0812

50% Off your next SAPCOOKBOOK order

If you plan of placing an order for 10 or more books from www.sapcookbook.com you qualify for volume discounts. Please send an email to books@sapcookbook.com or phone 951-788-0810 to place your order.

You can also fax your orders to 951-788-0812

Interview books are great for cross-training

In the new global economy, the more you know the better. The sharpest consultants are doing everything they can to pick up more than one functional area of SAP. Each of the following Certification Review / Interview Question books provides an excellent starting point for your module learning and investigation. These books get you started like no other book can – by providing you the information that you really need to know, and fast.

SAPCOOKBOOK Interview Questions, Answers, and Explanations

ABAP - SAP ABAP Certification Review: SAP ABAP Interview Questions, Answers, and Explanations

SD - SAP SD Interview Questions, Answers, and Explanations

Security - SAP Security: SAP Security Essentials

HR - mySAP HR Interview Questions, Answers, and Explanations: SAP HR Certification Review

BW - SAP BW Ultimate Interview Questions, Answers, and Explanations: SAW BW Certification Review

SAP SRM Interview Questions Answers and Explanations

Basis - SAP Basis Certification Questions: Basis Interview Questions, Answers, and Explanations

MM - SAP MM Certification and Interview Questions: SAP MM Interview Questions, Answers, and Explanations

SAP BW Ultimate Interview Questions, Answers, and Explanations

Key Topics Include

• The most important BW settings to know
• BW tables and transaction code quick references
• Certification Examination Questions
• Extraction, Modeling and Configuration
• Transformations and Administration
• Performance Tuning, Tips & Tricks, and FAQ
• Everything a BW resource needs to know before an interview

mySAP HR Interview Questions, Answers, and Explanations

Key topics include:

• The most important HR settings to know
• mySAP HR Administration tables and transaction code quick references
• SAP HR Certification Examination Questions
• Org plan, Compensation, Year End, Wages, and Taxes
• User Management, Transport System, Patches, and Upgrades
• Benefits, Holidays, Payroll, and Infotypes
• Everything an HR resource needs to know before an interview

SAP SRM Interview Questions, Answers, and Explanations

Key Topics Include

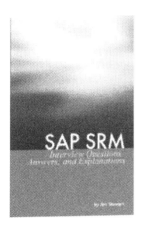

-The most important SRM Configuration to know
-Common EBP Implementation Scenarios
-Purchasing Document Approval Processes
-Supplier Self Registration and Self Service (SUS)
-Live Auctions and Bidding Engine, RFX Processes (LAC)
-Details for Business Intelligence and Spend Analysis
-EBP Technical and Troubleshooting Information

SAP MM Interview Questions, Answers, and Explanations

- The most important MM Configuration to know
- Common MM Implementation Scenarios
- MM Certification Exam Questions
- Consumption Based Planning
- Warehouse Management
- Material Master Creation and Planning
- Purchasing Document Inforecords

SAP SD Interview Questions, Answers, and Explanations

• The most important SD settings to know
• SAP SD administration tables and transaction code quick references
• SAP SD Certification Examination Questions
• Sales Organization and Document Flow Introduction
• Partner Procedures, Backorder Processing, Sales BOM
• Backorder Processing, Third Party Ordering, Rebates and Refunds
• Everything an SD resource needs to know before an interview

SAP Basis Interview Questions, Answers, and Explanations

• The most important Basis settings to know
• Basis Administration tables and transaction code quick references
• Certification Examination Questions
• Oracle database, UNIX, and MS Windows Technical Information
• User Management, Transport System, Patches, and Upgrades
• Backup and Restore, Archiving, Disaster Recover, and Security
• Everything a Basis resource needs to know before an interview

SAP Security Essentials

• Finding Audit Critical Combinations
• Authentication, Transaction Logging, and Passwords
• Roles, Profiles, and User Management
• ITAR, DCAA, DCMA, and Audit Requirements
• The most important security settings to know
• Security Tuning, Tips & Tricks, and FAQ
• Transaction code list and table name references

SAP Workflow Interview Questions, Answers, and Explanations

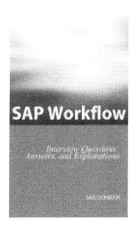

• Database Updates and Changing the Standard
• List Processing, Internal Tables, and ALV Grid Control
• Dialog Programming, ABAP Objects
• Data Transfer, Basis Administration
• ABAP Development reference updated for 2006!
• Everything an ABAP resource needs to know before an interview

SAP Business Workflow Interview Questions

www.ingramcontent.com/pod-product-compliance
Lightning Source LLC
Chambersburg PA
CBHW021144070326
40689CB00043B/1123